GIRL, YOU ARE WORTH EVERY NUGGET

LENNIE ALLS-VENNING

authorHOUSE®

AuthorHouse™
1663 Liberty Drive
Bloomington, IN 47403
www.authorhouse.com
Phone: 1 (800) 839-8640

Published by AuthorHouse 06/14/2017

ISBN: 978-1-5246-9663-4 (sc)
ISBN: 978-1-5246-9662-7 (e)

Library of Congress Control Number: 2017909342

Print information available on the last page.

I dedicate this book to my granddaughter Skylar Alysse McCray, who was born premature at 1 pound 6 ounces. When I first laid eyes on her, I immediately called her "my little nugget." As tiny as she was, I knew she would grow to be a priceless gift to the world, and she has become just that over eight years later. The day she was born, I stood there and wanted so desperately to do everything I could to help her – yet I was limited. All I could offer her was my love and lots of prayers. I began to think of every word of God that I could have applied to her situation, and I spoke it over her; I believe it was the power of those words, along with faith, that caused her to grow up into the young lady that she is today. I had vowed that she would know the power that worked in her. She would know that because of "The Word" of Jesus Christ that she is valuable. He has empowered her to triumph every time, even if it may look like defeat. She was not the only little nugget there that evening, and my prayer was that they all would make it. My prayer was that not only will my little nugget fully know her worth but also that the other female nuggets of the world will know theirs as well. God has poured into me nuggets that would empower each young girl.

ACKNOWLEDGMENTS

If I were to do as my heart leads, my acknowledgements would be a chapter on their own. However, as this book has taken me away into much prayer and dedication, I must show gratitude to my husband Raymond Venning Jr. I thank you for understanding even when you probably did not understand. I Thank you for the times you had to prepare your own meals, load the washer/dryer, and do all of the others things I so graciously do for you - You are one in a million. Thank you for pouring into this book with so much support; God sees every selfless labor of love, and He is rewarding you. No man can do anything unless He imparts, so all honor goes to God. I am humbled that he has chosen me to serve in this capacity. All the glory belongs to God.

PRAYER

Father God in the name of Jesus, I offer this prayer for your daughters. They are all miracles. Miracles because we know that the enemy desires to take the first breath they have inhaled, yet you kept them covered because you had a plan for their lives. I declare that every promise will be fulfilled in their lives. Father, you knew her before she was formed in her mother's womb. You knew her color, size, and shape; you knew everything about her, from the color of her skin to the shaping of her toes. I believe that when you decided on how much melanin she would have, you smiled and said, "yes, this is good." I believe that when you decided if she was going to be short or tall, you smiled and said, "Yes, this is good." I believe that when you decided on her frame, you smiled - once again - and said, "Yes, this is good." Father, when you had made every decision in creating your daughter, I believe you gleamed with the expectation of her one day looking into the mirror and saying, "I am fearfully and wonderfully made in His image, and marvelous is the works of His hands. Yes, He made me and everything he made is good." Now father, I pray that there will never be a time that your daughter looks into the mirror and sees less. Your daughter will always know that she is valuable because she is of a royal priesthood. Father, you told me if I make a decree in your name it shall be established, so I declare that your daughter will follow the steps that have been ordered just for her that will lead to a future of hope. Father, I declare that these lives will please you and reveal your word. I declare vessels that will live according to Your word. They are shielded from premature death; no affliction will dwell in them. I declare every negative thought that has been planned for her to be cancelled. Every plot and plan of Satan's are to be destroyed. The voice of Satan will forever be silent in Jesus' name, amen.

PREFACE

I am often reminded of a childhood cartoon *Popeye The Sailor*. He was what we call scrawny compared to his opposing Bluto. What strikes me most, if I remember correctly, is that Popeye always had what he needed on hand – and how spinach fortified and empowered him in every battle. Though it was fiction, even as a child I always wondered, why he waited until he was in the fight and near defeat to reach for his spinach. I remember as a child when I would scream at the television - as if he could hear - for him to take out his spinach and swallow it whole, as surely a fight with Bluto was near. Pop-eye always kept the spinach in his pocket. It wasn't a one-time fix, as he had to continuously feast on it, and as I recall he never left home without it. Though there were times that even while in the battle it was a struggle for him to grab the spinach, but he always managed to finally get his hands on it. There were even times when he had to endure a few punches possible defeat, but he never was because he knew where his strength lied: it came from the spinach. In a real world, he probably would've been warned of this big and bad Bluto, and he would've been prepared for the encounter.

Bluto wanted what Popeye had and was out to rob Pop-eye of what was most valuable to him: his lady. In a perfect world, one would think that because Bluto was bigger, Popeye would have no chance of victory.

God's purpose for each of us is that we know who we are in Him regardless of our statue. We are greater than anything that comes to oppose us and like Popeye, who used the spinach to empower, God is our strength and after we have come into a covenant with Him, we become empowered, too. We grow in strength the more we consume Him by way of The Word. He reminds us in John 10:10, that the thief's purpose is "...to steal, kill, and destroy'; my purpose is to give them a rich and satisfying life." You are inclusive of them. Yes, you personally! Yes, you specifically! He is talking about you, yes, you! There is a life of more than enough waiting just for you. There is a greater life for you.

He has come now to enlighten and remind you of whom you are in Him. Let each nugget of wisdom fortify you for the race; Let them be the answers to the lies the enemy tries to offer, and let them be the marrow of your being to produce the fruits of the spirit, while He looks at you to say, "You are good, my nugget." Hide each nugget in your heart, and if need be, put it in your pocket so that you won't ever answer to less than the precious jewels that you all are.

What you have in you is enough to conquer every opposition; pull it out and use it! Though one could wonder what good the spinach was, I believe it was his faith all along that prevailed.

YOU ARE UNCONQUERABLE: HE CALLS YOU A DIAMOND

For I can do all things through Christ who strengthens me.
—Philippians 4:13

Enduring love, strength, and commitment—yes, that's it. He loves you forever, and He's forever your strength. He's forever committed to you. You are unconquerable; that's what your name means in Greek. You are unconquerable because He conquered the cross for you. You have a multifaceted history dating back billions of years, and you are not the kind of girl to sit in a treasure chest. See, diamonds have beautified by day or shone in the night for ages. It warded off the vilest of spirits, and it wasn't afraid to go to battle as added protection or to be used as a weapon. You've even been used to heal wounds, way back when. You are sharper than any knife. You can't be broken. You are the most resilient of your kind.

They can't box you away for a particular use. You have a purpose, but it's not limited to a time. There is no limit to what you can do, for you can do all things through Christ.

Today, they say diamonds are a girl's best friend. We come in all shapes, sizes, and colors, but what makes us unique is our strength. We can be placed in any arena of any size, proportion, or color, but we have something that's unique: our strength and tenacity. You are eternal because He promises never to leave you or forsake you; you are strong even at your weakest point. He causes you to triumph over every obstacle. His strength causes you to confront and conquer all opposition. Though there will be counterfeits that are beautifully sized and composed, the true test will come when the heat is added. Regardless of the fiery blazes that may come, He will be with you. You have been launched from the deepest depths, but you landed with a purpose. You are an original. You cannot be duplicated because you are one of a kind. You are of like kind, His kind.

REFLECTIONS

YOU ARE A NATURAL: HE CALLS YOU A PEARL

For God so love the world that gave His only begotten that whosoever believeth in me, shall not perish but have everlasting life. John 3:16

Some have said that the very thing that housed you holds the power of life and death. When pearls were formed, they were formed in an oyster. During the Great Depression, oysters offered a source of protein (life), but it caused a bloodshed (death) during the Oyster Wars of the late 1800s.

So yes, He calls you a pearl, and because of Him you have that same power. **According to Proverbs 18:21, "The power of the tongue is life and death and those who love to talk will eat what**

it produces." Could we say then that even they knew He would call you a pearl?

There are lots of antiquity about your history. Irritants, parasites, and intruders are all unlikely words that are associated with your formation. Could we say then that the very same thing that may try to destroy you will be the very same thing used to prosper? It cannot be used against you—you know, those things that the devil will send to try to kill you. He will use these things to try to rob you of your inheritance and to suck life out of you. The things that will come to infect, frustrate, and hinder you will all work for your good. So, welcome it, because if it doesn't come, you can't achieve your purpose. You are equipped to produce the plan of God for your life. You are a rare find; you are perfectly sized, lustrous, and properly shaped for whatever comes your way. You are built for this. Some shun what housed you because of where you came from and your purpose, but He has a plan for my life. So, you see, it doesn't matter where I am from. Regardless of your past or where you are now, perhaps in the murkiest of places, there is value in you. There is greatness in you. You don't need others to see it because you know. You know who you are because there are few like you. Don't dare short-change yourself based on appearance. There is more to you than meets the eyes. The common eyes won't see your worth because your value is not in what the eyes behold—it's hidden in you. It was meant to keep the shallow-minded and vain culprits away. They put value on what is seen, but you can't be defined that way. You are a guarded treasure. He guards you with His life. He has equipped you with the ability to embrace the attacks and turn them into treasure. You will forever say, **"It was good that I was afflicted that I might know His statutes"** (**Psalm 119:71**). It will all work for your good so you say, "Take your best shot. I have been equipped. I have the best defense mechanism. I have Jesus. I have the Word."

REFLECTIONS

YOU CAN'T BE MARKED DOWN: HE CALLS YOU PRICELESS

And yet, O LORD, you are our Father. We are the clay, and you are the potter. We all are formed by your hand.
—Isaiah 64:8

Like diamonds, pearls and furs they are often changed and manipulated regardless of its euthenics to be something different than what God destined it to be. You were uniquely designed and cannot be change like things. You may hang with the rest, but you are valuable. To the untrained eye you may look the same, but to the eyes of those like me, you can be fully seen. You may be crammed among the rest, but even they know who you are. Although, you are made to stand out, sometimes your presence and your light are needed to enhance and promote your surroundings. Know your value and what you bring to the table. It does not matter if you are not given the recognition due. What truly matters is that you know, because if you don't, you will always be looking for someone to affirm your worth based on their standards. They can't affirm your worth because they didn't make you. You have been carefully molded- fearfully, wonderfully, and marvelously made. It took Him time to make you, so don't ever allow anyone to put a value on you.

When He was done making you, He looked at you and said, "priceless." Know your worth because you are forever in His hands; He is the reason that you are valuable. Your starting price is value, and you can never be priced lower than that. His plans are to make you prosper. Yes, because He said, **"For I have known the thoughts that I am thinking towards you—an affirmation of Jehovah; thoughts of peace, and not of evil, to give to you posterity and hope"** (Jeremiah 29:11).

Know that situations will come on purpose to devalue. Some people will come with a price on their lips and marker in their hands to lessen you. They won't recognize your worth because they don't know who you are. They won't recognize you because you don't look like what they are accustomed to. Know that you have to be careful because many will be intimidated by your worth. Some will not understand that you have been made to enhance their worth, but instead they will try to lessen you to make themselves more content. I believe they call that a wholesale. He has given you an MSRP. Yes, that's right—my manufacturer has suggested a price for me, and it is valuable. Now, real world retailers can reduce the MSRP once they have purchased the goods, but that does not apply to you because you cannot be purchased. You are not for sale. You were bought with a price that only He could have afforded to pay, and He paid it just for you!

REFLECTIONS

THAT'S NOT HOW IT ENDS:
HE CALLS YOU CLAY

Whenever a clay pot he was working on was ruined, he would
rework it into a new clay pot the way he wanted to make it.
—Jeremiah 18:4

Yes, that's it- you understand now? He knew you would not always get it right. He knew you would miss the mark sometimes and fall. Girl, He knew you would mess up more than once, so He calls you clay. He called you clay because He is the maker. Yes, it is true, and it is stated in **Isaiah 64:8: "And now, Jehovah, thou art our Father; we are the clay, and thou our potter; and we all are the work of thy hand."** He called you clay because you would forever be pliable, making it easy for you to be reshaped.

He knew you before you were known. He knew every mistake, every transgression, every blunder of your being. He knew it, so each day he holds you in His hands. Know there will be times because of your disobedience, that it will feel like He is not holding you, but those times will be His ways of disciplining. Oh, yes, He must discipline, because He truly loves you. For it will be like a parent that allows a child to fall knowing that when he gets up he will be wiser. You probably won't realize it when it happens but know that it will be for your good. Sometimes you will be separated from people that shouldn't be in your life; it is simply Him pruning and cutting away the things that have come to hinder you from reaching your goals.

See, He has a plan for your life and that's why He keeps you near the cross because each day unfolds that plan piece by piece. He knows what's ahead of you because remember He knew it well before it happens. Regardless of what it feels like, remember you are forever in His hands. Like a good book, your life may have many genres, containing mysteries, comedies, adventures, fantasies and even a few scary lines, but it's not over until He says it over. There will be people that will try to keep you in a certain chapter, but remind them, "Who me? Yes, I did that, but that's chapters ago. It may have been non-fiction but I'm no longer there. You need to keep reading. It won't end until His expected end. Don't believe me, read it for yourself. **For I know the thoughts that I think toward you, said the LORD, thoughts of peace, and not of evil, to give you an expected end, Jeremiah 29:1.**" You may have to remind yourself even, regardless of where you are in life that He's there. There is no depth to which He won't go to save you.

Psalms 139:1-1
O LORD, you have searched me and you know me.
You know when I sit and when I rise; you
perceive my thoughts from afar.

You discern my going out and my lying down;
you are familiar with all my ways.

Before a word is on my tongue you know it completely, O LORD.

You hem me in--behind and before; you
have laid your hand upon me.

Such knowledge is too wonderful for
me, too lofty for me to attain.

Where can I go from your Spirit? Where
can I flee from your presence?

If I go up to the heavens, you are there; if I make
my bed in the depths, ¹you are there.

If I rise on the wings of the dawn, if I
settle on the far side of the sea,

even there your hand will guide me, your
right hand will hold me fast.

If I say, "Surely the darkness will hide me and
the light become night around me,"

even the darkness will not be dark to you; the night will
shine like the day, for darkness is as light to you.

For you created my inmost being; you knit
me together in my mother's womb.

I praise you because I am fearfully and wonderfully made;
your works are wonderful; I know that full well.

LENNIE ALLS-VENNING

My frame was not hidden from you when I was made in the secret place. When I was woven together in the depths of the earth,

your eyes saw my unformed body. All the days ordained for me were written in your book before one of them came to be.

How precious to me are your thoughts, O
God! How vast is the sum of them!

REFLECTIONS

WATCH OUT HERE SHE COME, YOU GO GIRL! ... ... HE CALLS YOU PROMISE

Every square inch on which you place your foot will be yours. Your borders will stretch from the wilderness to the mountains of Lebanon, from the Euphrates River to the Mediterranean Sea. No one will be able to stand in your way. Everywhere you go, God-sent fear and trembling will precede you, just as he promised. Deuteronomy 11:24-25

Every day you wake up, you are closer to the fulfillment of purpose for your life. Whether you walk or run, it takes you closer. You have territories to cover, and you must cover them because in you lies the answer that many have been waiting for. Oh, know there will be days you won't feel like running and other days that you won't even feel like moving, but because of the prize that's before you, you cannot stop. He has prepared a way of escape for every opposition. He's with you, so don't be afraid regardless of the heights or the depth. Before you can be pitfalls that you may very well fall in, en route to what He's promised. Oh, but know in your walk, echoes from the pits will scream your name but don't look back. Your past will forever desire to be a part of your future, but it no longer belongs. Your past was necessary in order to get you to your destiny. You had to go through things along the journey and you will continue to walk forward, for you were not made to walk backwards. Your feet are pointed ahead and you must follow.

Every stop, every glimpse back, will only slow the process. You are moving forward lighter than ever. You cannot bring things from your past, for it will only make the journey harder. Do not forget what He's done for you. See your mistakes as your opponent, regardless of how close it gets to you, don't let it get ahead of you.

Many anticipate the victory after each encounter, but Oh, you are victory. You won't wait for it to be called at the end, you are victorious going in. You carry the title; it is yours and you wear it well. It has been branded by every stripe He took, and He took it just for you. Many will be confused, because of your past, but that is behind you where it belongs and promise is before you, where you belong. He's promised! **"When you go out to battle against your enemies and see horses and chariots and people more numerous than you, do not be afraid of them; for the LORD your God, who brought you up from the land of Egypt, is with you," Deuteronomy 20:1.**

REFLECTIONS

GOD SAID YOU HAVE WHAT IT TAKES: HE CALLS YOU PURE

How can a young person keep his life pure? [He can do it] by holding on to your word. Psalms 119:9

Yes, that's right He calls you pure. You are pure. He calls it because He knew you. He knew your heart before it made its first beat. He called you pure, but not as the world calls it. He knew if you would abstain or if you wouldn't. He has given you a way of escape, with His Word. He knew you before you were conceived, and he knew the foolishness of your heart. It's in The Word, **"A child's heart has a tendency to do wrong, but the rod of discipline removes it far away from him," Proverbs 22:15**. He knew what you would have to contend with; He knew it all. He knew every battle you would endure for your independence well before you were ready. You were created in His image, but He knew there would be battles while you are maturing physically, as well as sexually. He understood the peer pressure, and how you would battle to keep your friends. Oh, and let's not forget the fads that will be here today and gone tomorrow. He knew that you would sometimes fight just to be accepted- because truly who wants to be left out?

He knew with all of it would come confusion, but He gave you His word. **"Be not afraid, for with thee I am, look not around, for I am thy God, I have strengthened thee, Yea, I have helped thee, yea, I upheld thee, With the right hand of My righteousness," Isaiah 41:10.**

Oh, don't be fooled because temptation will come to change your confession. Paul said it best, **"So, I discover this principle: When I want to do, what is good, evil is with me," Romans 7:21.** Nevertheless, you hold fast to His word. There is always a chance you might fall, but you will not remain down. It will not change the fact that He calls you pure though, for His blood never loses its power, and you are forever redeemed by it. It cleanses from all transgressions; it makes you new. Believe it because it is written in Isaiah 44:22 and holds true for you, **"I have blotted out your transgressions like a cloud and your sins like mist; return to, for I have redeemed you."** Oh, and remember you are forever in His hands and He calls you pure, despite how the world calls it. You are pure because His blood washes you white as snow.

REFLECTIONS

GOD SAYS YOU ARE BEAUTIFUL:
He Calls You Beautiful!!

For you created my inmost being; you knit me together in my mother's womb. I praise you because I am fearfully and wonderfully made; your works are wonderful; I know that full well. – Psalm 139:13-14

Don't ever doubt you are the apple of His eye. Yes, of course you know it, but it is nevertheless good to hear it. If no one ever says it again, still you heard it from Him first. He called you beautiful and when you look in the mirror, you should see you as He sees you. When you are having a bad hair day, you will see it. You may gain a scar here and there, but still, you will see it.

Cookies, cakes, and creams may add a few pounds, but you will see it. You are forever beautiful, because He doesn't lie. He knew you long before you were conceived. He knew you then, as you are now and He still called you beautiful. He has done a remarkable work in shaping you, from your forehead to your toes. You should see it and say, "Marvelous is the works of His hands. I see His wonderful works in me. I see the beauty He sees. I have been remarkably made by Him!" Some will point out what they call "imperfections", but God is perfect, so imperfections they are not. They will try to show you, but you will never see it the way they do, for you will know very well His craftsmanship, and there are no filters needed.

REFLECTIONS

YOU SHALL LIVE AND NOT DIE:
HE CALLS YOU A CAMELLIA

**I will not die, but live, and tell of the works
of the LORD, Psalms 118:17**

Yes, that's right a camellia. You are forever clothed in beauty, regardless of the season. You bloom in the most unlikely seasons. When you should be withering, He sustains you. The briskest of air cannot steal your shine, because that's when you produce and show what you are made of. During the dampest of seasons, you are forever shining. When all around you things are falling, you are not moved, for you will forever shine. Yes, He calls you a camellia because He knew quite well what life held for you, but He has made you to shine regardless of what life brings- regardless of the seasons. We all will have seasons, but He has created you to live. You are sustained by Him. It's true because it is in the word, **"And he shall be like a tree planted by streams of water, that brength forth its fruit in its season, and whose leaf doth not wither; And in whatsoever he doeth he shall prosper, Psalms 1:3.** All you have to do is remain fortified with His word. His word is life; he died so that you may live. Like a body that needs food to live, your soul shall forever desire every morsel of His words. You shall live and not die.

I am the living bread that came down from heaven. Whoever eats this bread will live forever. This bread is my flesh, which I will give for the life of the world," John 6:51.

LET THERE BE LIFE!!

Inhaling and exhaling are clear indication of life, by the taking in and the releasing of life. Speaking the Word breathes the breath of Life, a Life that releases Life (the promises of God.) Breathe the breath of Life, until every withered place is no more.
Lennie Venning

The thief's purpose is to steal and kill and destroy. My purpose is to give them a rich and satisfying life. John 10:10

REFLECTIONS

HE LOVES YOU, HE LOVES YOU, NOT ... LIKE THE WORLD: HE CALLS YOU HIS LOVE

I have loved you with an everlasting love; I have drawn you with loving-kindness. – Jeremiah 31:3

He loves you, and unlike the world with its conditions, His love for you is not predicated on your actions. His love is everlasting and steadfast. His love is not hesitant. He loves you even when you do not love yourself. He loves you even when you are not lovable. He loves you even in the darkest of times. You cannot exhaust His love, for it doesn't run out. He loves you enough to discipline you because He only wants what is best for you. His love wins every time.

You will forever be one with Him. He gave His life for you while knowing that there would be times you would love the world more than Him. There is no greater love than this. The world could never love like He loves, because His love is constant, and you do not have to do anything to earn it.

So how could you not love Him despite knowing that He loved you first? How could you not give yourself to Him when He gave His life for you? Give yourself to the One that loves you, again unlike the world- no conditions needed. He fulfilled the conditions for your love way back at Calvary, when He suffered and died for you. Love the One that calls you His love.

REFLECTIONS

FREE TIDBITS

- Never apologize for not settling. You owe nothing to anyone, but you owe yourself everything.

- Live unapologetically in your worth. Never apologize for where He's taking you. Being true to your identity is required to get you through the doors to your destiny. You deny that, and you are giving up your destiny.

- Have a "take it or leave it" posture on your worth, and never settle for a markdown.

- Never reduce yourself for another. People who are uncomfortable with your gifts and talents are not the people for you.

- When you deny your gifts, you are actually telling God that you'd much rather not have them.

- Your gifts may make you feel uncomfortable, but you should value them because your gifts have been given to you for a purpose.

- Your gifts are not for everyone, and the ones that cannot accept your gifts really aren't accepting of you, either; it's a package deal.

- You are valuable; be certain to not be cheated. You were made to prosper. Live your lives as gain. You add, if they are adding. You multiply, but only if they are adding. You subtract, if they are adding. You divide as long as they add. Together, you can become a fraction of each other that makes one whole.

Printed in the United States
By Bookmasters